SIN EATER

SIN EATER

ANGELA HIBBS

ARP BOOKS · WINNIPEG

ARP BOOKS (Arbeiter Ring Publishing)
201E-121 Osborne Street
Winnipeg, Manitoba
Canada R3L 1Y4
arpbooks.org

Printed in Canada by Kromar Printing on paper with 50% PCW
Cover image by Mary St-Amand Williamson
Design by Relish New Brand Experience Inc.

ARP acknowledges the financial support of the Government of Canada through the Canada Book Fund for our publishing activities.

ARP acknowledges the support of the Province of Manitoba through the Book Publishing Tax Credit and of Manitoba Culture, Heritage, and Tourism through the Book Publisher Marketing Assistance Program.

We acknowledge the support of the Canada Council for our publishing program.

With the generous support of the Manitoba Arts Council.

We would like to acknowledge funding support from the Ontario Arts Council, an agency of the Government of Ontario.

LIBRARY AND ARCHIVES CANADA CATALOGUING IN PUBLICATION

Hibbs, Angela, 1978-, author
        Sin eater / Angela Hibbs.

Poems.
ISBN 978-1-894037-49-5 (pbk.)

        I. Title.

PS8615.I33S55 2014   C811'.6   C2014-900178-9

For Rob Kingston

I have
no master but always wonder,
what is making my master sad?
—Matthew Zapruder

FOREWORD

IN WHICH SIN REPLACES CULTURE

—a translation of T.S. Eliot's *Notes Towards the Definition of Culture*

If we take sin seriously, we see that a people do not need
    merely *enough*.
Sin may even be described simply as that which makes life
    worth living.

Fortunate the man who, at the right moment, commits the
right sin; fortunate also the man who at the right moment
displays the right virtue.

A people should be neither too prideful nor too prone to
anger, if its culture is to flourish.

A society requires not only a body of politicians who knows
what is being done, but also a body of sinners who knows
what to do.

sloth

                    her country tongue
and country heart anaesthetized and mute
with labor.
—Rhina P. Espaillat

Please enjoy this music while your call is redirected.

THE NEAR FUTURE

I will be an envelope,
a mouth
that expands.

I will raise
the appropriate
hand.

On request,
I will become obsolete.
The repercussions percuss

my chest.
The most active
I am

is in forgetting.
Encouraging
myself to forget.

ERSATZ KITCHEN

Divide lunch from work, from other lunches.
Natural as canned tuna.

Other people's butter.
I self-slather. Exult.

Three accountants chant Hockey
stats. The plant lady's green
watering cans overflow.

A stranger's birthday cake: its stale,
stale body consoles.

The lunch bags open: private worship stations
last night's time capsules.
Food disappears into mouths
then toilets. All these cubbies. How we shelter.
Digest in peace.

The fridge will save us all!

HOLDING IT TOGETHER

I punch the circular hole
into the plastic squares
that hold bread bags together.

Tom marks the date on the tabs.
It is understood the date means expiration.

I bring beets to work. My favourite
sound: spoon in glass

cylinder. Tom never
calls in sick. Doesn't happen.

He doesn't want anyone marking dates
but him. Tom's name on his locker: all caps.

Every day I throw today away.

THE REALITY CHECKLIST

Most grounding: flavour of apples.
Beware too waxy. Just waxy enough. Is real.

Confirm litter box's lack of arrangement.

Distrust overabundance of exclamation points!

Some whispers will be inaudible. Check.
Not all. Most.

"That's unreal!" may be heard in the real.

Tense spider-looking hands:
without further evidence: the unreal in the real.

Lights don't always work: could be either.
Trains late: same.

Doubt the easily replicated: spanakopita,
too gluey. Still. A recipe error not proof enough
for an audience with the Reality board.

Clouds may mock the brain's shape
or the shape the brain is expected to take.
Note: exposed brain may lose form. In reality.
Slosh.

Listen! For click of glass on metal
finding that, ensure it sounds
different than glass on wood, blunt, not chime.

If ten people in a row have a sister
doubt the authenticity of their humanity.

Fields do not long to be beheld:
indifference is characteristic of reality.

Seeing all that is said as transcript:
false alarm.

Violins in torture chambers
may be a soundtrack. Disorientation
gathers in the real as much as the unreal.

If you wish you were somewhere else
reality may be upon you.

*This checklist is under construction.

**Unreal checkmarks should outnumber real.

***Refrain from using formulas for the real;
    unknowns function differently in the unreal.

TRUE OR FALSE SHARK

Clasped, shark unbudges.
Shark is out of water for a week
without signs of rot.
Shark is on sale at your local big box.
Shark smells like a condom, a CD, a prescription
pill bottle. The shark is willing to pose in crime
scene reenactments. The shark is composed
of up to 20% fire retardants. The shark does not protest
donning gown and mortarboard.
If the shark has waited while you've consulted
this checklist.

CRAZY TRAIN: A DIAGNOSTIC CHECKLIST

What makes the train crazy?

When did you first notice the train was crazy?

Is it only the train's behavior that makes it crazy? Do the tracks or décor or other passengers contribute to your impression of craziness?

What would a train that is not crazy be like?

Have you ever been on a train that you would describe as "not crazy"?

Would the train continue to be crazy if it were no longer on the rails?

Did you purchase a ticket on the train?

Can you locate an exit on the train?

Is it foreseeable that the train's behavior could change?

Under what conditions would the train be endurable?

Are there other responses available to you besides fear?

Does the train remind you of anything?

Does the train remind you of anyone?

FORMULA (FOR EVERYTHING)

holds those variables that resist tighter.

Air excluded from formula for everything
predicts not *where*
you'll spit but the shape
it will fall in. Calculates which button
falls first from a blazer.

The formula makes meteorology a sham.

The formula knows, based on age and religion,
who will believe in it most.

The formula reckons the ripples in rivers
where stones are skipped,
determines duration of manias and fads
assesses probability of Jumpers jumping

from bridges. Drunk on surfeit of certainty
leads to excessive jaywalking.
Also, benefits the consumer economy.
Predict and prevent as necessary.

POEM IN PLACE OF A TRIP TO NIAGARA FALLS

Rock-stranded
she did not think about the backyard rocks
used to play mermaid.

She thought of rescue. A rope.
Or a man with arms like one.

The helicopter released a lawn chair.

The chair's crisscross fabric created a multitude
of frames through which to view the falls.

AUDIENCE 'TIL I DIE

i
the day that nielsen left

I asked myself
who cares?

I asked myself
who is watching?
Who is measuring?

I kept my own journal
and, like most, it would be
unread. Irrelevant.

What would I say was its purpose?

To be my memory.

I arranged Christmas lights
as an understudy
to Nielsen,
as a pacifier.

No company. No watcher.

ii
coping with the box

Nielsen, I have taken to listening to my neighbour's TV
through the wall. I use a juice glass. You will never know
what this 18 to 49 year-old watches.

If I watch on mute, you should leave it unaccounted.

iii
cross viewing

Secret viewing.
Unmeasured slices of story,
rule-stripped sport.

> To the sports bar. A bribe
> to watch *Nip/Tuck*
> without Nielsen.
> Sweeter.

iv
commercial

Stuff a pain receptor
with Tylenol
with Gravol
with Herbal Remedy
so suspect.
Stuff it. Snuff it.

> This commercial cost more than my house.
> It shelters me just as well.

V

notes towards a mission statement

1.

What we said about you before
was not a lie,
just a little fuzzy.

A Chinese tattoo meaning strange
rather than mysterious. A stroke away.
We work hard to measure you better.

2.

inexact still has exact in it
untruth, truth.

it is not that we didn't want to see you
it is that we could not see you.

3.

Consider truth a spectrum
with neither pole habitable.
No oxygen, no food, the like.

Think of a kiss's distance
from full blown infidelity.
Compare a glass of beer
and a keg.

So much more to the body than lips.
So many more bubbles.

What we said about you
had some bubbles in it.

pride

THE SORROW MACHINE

sensed lies.
Charted blood pressure
against serotonin.
Derived fractals from frowns.

Years passed, we were fervent,
designing machines to quantify
our misery.

New hormones we pierced with our flags,
naming them after you and me in turns.

Your extravagant sorrow descriptions—
you wrote small, filled margins, turned pages.
The machine didn't cotton to them.
Adjectives too much effort for The Miserable.

Something in the way I pressed my pencil
ranking my mood a zero
weighed more than yours.

My grief scored three full points
higher than yours.

for David McGimpsey

You left to quantify happiness.
None of the sorrow gauges
were applicable.

The machine is noisy.
The bottle of how you used to smell
is almost empty. In the toilet
my Kleenex blossomed.

DAWN DEVICE

gauges eye flutters per second
weighs pillow pools
accounts for eyebrow battles and
linen disarray.
Porous tongue sands granola,
sloshes milk. Dawn device
measures dispersal
of sugars through tongue.
Blood. All stored by lunch
when dawn device breaks
publishes its prediction for the day.

for Jason Camlot

JESUS' UNDERSTUDY

applied on a lark. One interviewer
requested, will you
grow a beard?

Ya, ya, he 'sured them, eager
to move on to the tough questions.
He failed to anticipate
the loneliness for his own face.

All jobs take time to get used to.
So the groomers assured him.
Jesus' house was full of cold shoulders.
Neither servant, master, nor peer.

Days off did not arrive. Jesus
was first sick, then on leave, then AWOL.
Concerns expressed for his labour rights
were deemed selfish. They said he had gall.

Forty days in the desert is more awful
when it's against your will.
Not so much as a minor demon
bothering to dog you.

Hands cut on cactus needles.

for Kathryn Mockler

FLOOD

Water laps the eighth floor window
it is only the lake forgetting it has been reclaimed.

So much for reaping what you've sown.
Those for sidewalk sweeping known

are quick to take up nets
and clear any leaves from their plots.

Writing a will seemed too grim.
Where you used to walk, you'll swim.

JESSICA

The well swallowed you; you sang fables.
What accident put lure into your name?
You who were trapped unlure-able
under what hard stuff the world is made.
Gravity took you for an example,
cloaked for days in unexplained shade.
Absence as souvenir: your lost toe.
Dubbed "everybody's baby"
before you were old enough to veto.
A warning to so many,
a threat to babies of fewer owners.
Your mother a minor,
neighbours had to tsk.
You sirened miners
to a near impossible task.
Flash made daylight dim.
Your first photographer
Pulitzer laureled. Right
place, right time, your
own opposite.

PERSEPHONE

made her mother
deal with the devil.
Whose fallow period is the world's
fallow.

My own affairs with minor demons
shame me.

LIGHT DETECTION

The shine off a sail
unlights the room
neighbours a yellow oval
on an off-yellow boom

refuses to be missed.
White rectangle bisects brown rectangle.
Orange, white, purple and black mist
makes its impression, tangible.

A colon is a left hook and right jab.
A bracket is the West wind.
A period wants no drop more than a dab…
Three pennies line up for an ellipsis.

The above weather known as nipply,
(perhaps just colloquially)
rectangles repeat without introduction
a line is fine but a wall is obstruction.

greed

LIGHT DETECTIVE

Boom boom boom
raps a yellow oval into the door.

Which room, which sale?
The oval will not disappear.

Impossible to fail
P.I. axes syntax

to tax the synapse
to the brink of collapse.

Leave stranger weather a stranger.
Our uncouth sleuth claims a booth,

picks his tooth, eyes a busker pollute
the silence with his flute. Whose flute?

Likely his own. Our dick stays mute.
He 'as nudding but achs for silent h's.

In a polling booth he first uttered,
"In vermouth truth."

The detective daytrades
adverbs for adjectives,

refuses to go unpaid.
His preferred rectangles are legal tender.

Untender, his methods.
Whither a door without a floor?

Let it wither. He undeals in metaphors.

He takes on a case, top secret
the privacy of the dick emphasized.

Top refers primarily to its position
on his desk. His time by him alone prized.

Though none are curious,
tell the details, he shant.

His own view never in doubt.
The five w's populate his mant

ra. The evidence: a sail, unlighting a room,
avoided the passive voice by a hair.

for Angela Szczepaniak

CHOOSE YOUR FAVOURITE SHAPE

"As beggars entertain and nurse their lice."
—Kunitz's translation of Baudelaire's *Au Lecteur*

In scriptures inspiration comes from nature. A hill, a fire.
How can we entertain our lice? The translator unexplains. Or,
the translation is the explanation. Ex the x.
Plains, planes, sands, flattens. A desert atmosphere.

The dream that reveals all is impossible
to recall. Pass the town that broke down
drivers stop in. Ignorance often excuses ingratitude.
      Important shoes
were more memorable than the occasion they were worn to.

What else to build in a desert
but a pyramid. The stables are sinking. This is
a big event to a stranger or two.
Nobody showed up to mourn the death of curiosity.

Old buildings are reassuring. Time heals all
but words stay impenetrable.

THE BOHEMIANS

They say people are still having sex.
They mean the bohemians.

Fabrics, pretty for reasons I cannot figure,
fade on their flopping walls.

I don't fit in with the bohemians.
I can't stay in bed long enough.
My record was three days.
I become vertical
as if involuntarily.

Their ice cream is largely butterscotch.
Lovers, lazy in all but loving, lick
the lines their drippy scoops leave.

I kept forgetting the butterscotch.
Nobody licks the sugar trails from my chin.

The bohemians are not taking any meetings.
They have no magazine.
Their crooked hands conceal their sketches.
They have exposed underwear, uneven haircuts.

ALL OF THE GIRLS

One had the best hair, another
the best backpack. All of the girls
wanted to be Alyssa

Milano. Magazines revealed the steps
she took to be herself. They memorized
these steps.

All of the girls she knew wrote books
dedicated to their mothers.
The girls she knew

kept kitten-covered, tiny-locked diaries.
There she existed. When they were women
the kittens evaporated and the diaries were journals.
Still she existed.

They all gave themselves divorces, and legal agreements
that divvied up their children's days. They idolized
more age appropriate celebrities who also received
child support. They started second families. They turned out

to be reruns of the first. Their second books were not
dedicated to their mothers.
Not overtly.

POLITE, CONVENTION-RIDDEN SOCIETIES

with lines from reviews on CinemaClock.com

A laser of storytelling is violating you
like watching a train wreck in slow motion.
Leaving you, sympathetic, sensitive, disturbed and generally
    vulnerable.
It is however pointless, slow, boring.

A great movie to hear patrons' popcorn crunching
so intriguing to decipher: a cinematic salad
that may cause emotional indigestion.
A reflection on today's society. Artistic. Thus,

I loved the movie and the cast.
A form of despair: how original to see! It takes you
to the bones! Don't make it a turtle convention.
A very potent symbiosis of histrionics.

It is a work of art that irreverently imitates life
and the many emotions that men do not or cannot
usually protest about in polite, convention-ridden societies.
It captured the New York tension between people and
    Melancholy.

If you expect to be spoon-fed, then forget it, this isn't a film
    for you.
If you like movies with likeable characters this isn't the film
    for you.
If you're expecting a porn fest, you shouldn't go to see it.

FORMULA FOR WINTER

Limp hosed hosers hose lawn hard
at night and on & on.

Across the winter yard, they hawk.
They gawk. The young swirl.

Figure eighters orbit.
Watchers dream

invitations indoors.
Should their traps go unfilled

they blame winter's brevity.

LAW OF SIMILARITY

A cow and his jacket are soon parted.
Sometimes a cow is just his jacket
draped over a sawhorse. The cow's hair shines,
suggests light. Skyscrapers reflect the sun. A beau

sees himself in his beloved's bun.
Polished windows. The sun dreams it is a tower
made of hair. Leather's thickness
is gauged for uniformity.

The gauge recalls the calipers used to measure
human body fat. The commercial
shows when shampoo is applied—
hair strands beef up.

Fattened before slaughter; peel pelt from thickest
part of leg. Skins are bathed
in tree bark, water, and vegetable extract
to make leather resist water. Your grandmother was wrong:

cows are not waterproof.
The stamping we learned:
pre-cut leather bands seared
with heated metal; our wrists ringed

in souvenir. In death,
your grandmother's hair will live on
in wigs. Sold in the mirrored tower on Crescent Street.
The crescent moon a template

for the smile of one fitted with the hair.
Of course handbags are carried like spears.
Skin piles, all of us.

You should be redirected to the next section shortly.

gluttony

BARIATRIC SURGERY *a poem in two courses*

I

Contemplate the operation; munch tripe
Finish your plate
This informational video provided
with industrial music in the background

Bariatric surgery with calming piano sonatas—
intestinal diasporas, tunnels tunnel, pouches pouched,
    clamps clamped, created a cut,
a cutting for spy-cam penetration

Gloved hands displace the liver
reinforce the staple
divert digestive river

prevent breathing
make that, bleeding
jujunum—

juju gums
Line up the edges of the intestine
smooth and even

Two open windows, one pro ana, one chubby chasers
Bariatric surgery with calming curried potatoes—

Symptoms may not be associated with surgery.
The FDA may later forbid what she had done.
Should your internal organs break the law, take comfort,

they are invisible. Maybe she will consult her physician.
Maybe that was he, driving thru ahead of her.
The Doctor performs

a bariatric surgery on himself.
Bariatric surgery with soothing parsley frittatas—

2

HEALING

"Chew up your food good. Four ounces maximum. Can't
    eat Nachos from Taco Bell no more."

Mega describes the donuts or the box they nest in.
Also, the value.

The writers or the dieters put the industry in "diet industry."
Some writers are prophets:
they take dictation from those who require
no more than nine teaspoons of food a day.

Calorie counters consume corn by the kernel.

Maybe the only organ communicating
with her brain was her stomach. Maybe try a tapeworm.
There are those who consider the stomach
the "other brain." Are the brain and the stomach one?
Bariatric surgery with calming piano sonatas—
Bariatric sundaes with salted peanut bananas—

NECTARINE

What resists is skin
what breaks the skin is teeth
the sandy texture, the seeds.

A choking hazard or grow
a sidewalk
tree.

Juice on hands
transferred to text
tiles, to turns
tiles.

for Melissa A. Thompson

FRANCIS BACON'S STUDIO

Though unclothed
this body resembles nothing more than a pile of laundry

HP sauce mixed in
            powdered chicken soup
with a palette knife
            tastes alarming
-ly like steak

Sometimes the sick must drink oil
and soy sauce, to keep from fading away to

When too long has passed without sleep
Sleeping pills

grogginess is better than what it prevents

Flashed a light in his eyes
to make himself produce

CAST IRON PAN

Expect klunk. Crystal clang. Echo of bang.
The cast iron pan rises. Shrinks. Swells.

Thud. Expect lead. Figure full metal. A full metal jacket.
Examine: full and metal and jacketed. Collision. Study
new leaves. Turn them over.
In the after, jackets and crystal.

Ground into the ground;
a fine woman is ground fine. Hear crystal
ring. Hear fistfall whistle.
Sound jabs eardrum; waves curve.
Collision.

Excite full metal impact. Heavy
hands make faces heavy. Pull
face from floor. Surrender
leaves hands unscathed. Sling jaw into place. Wrap
temples. Collect teeth from concrete.
Shards ground into the ground.
Scrub bloodstains from concrete. Stare
as blood exits. Gushes become seeps. Waste time.

Root canal expected to follow
impact. Shrug the thought. Be
full metal.

MILK

It's a movie about a movie. In it milk
stands in for thirst. A truck
hauls a car; the car: milk. Later,
the milk, older but unsoured.

The unspoiled spoils of the milkmaid's toil pool
in and out of glass or roll into the ditch
of the mouth, onto floor. Repeat. Don't cry
when it dives, from the top of the fridge. Don gloves.

No, don *blue* gloves, those that stretch to the elbow
joint. Location change: the barman offers *The milk
of Christ?* Likely heard wrong.

In a climactic scene, floodlights illuminate a milk-flood.
Then, the night sky is a jigsaw of blackbirds
who split to reveal a day sky. Today, more milk than blue.

for Katherine Crossman

lust

BONES

I take dictation from one.
I have taken note of its intake
of light; the nose receives, the temples
reject. My penetrability
inverted. I have been made light,
dining with him. His two cents
not contributed. Alone
responsible for the
definition of our relationship.

I have not thanked my thumb
for holding the pen
or the skull for his company.
A keepsake. A word that has
yet to be invented. A paperweight.

The light has erased my arm. I hold
the skull and resist
breaking what I cannot repair.

The satiation of my desire
was its cessation. Only skull
has counted the brushstrokes
made in the black. Light neglects
ferns. Ferns are trampled.

THE FITZGERALDS ON LEAVE

They dawdled over coffee, loitered over wine. Laid

rolls to waste before an indifferent clock.

Her chair teetered between two stairs; food fled her plate.

Her face a dish he sent back.

She pinned infidelities to his lapel. He brushed them off
like ashes.

Even at starting a fight: impotent. Public toilets afforded
her minutes of privacy.

She collected wet coins. Pondered the year of their minting.

He insisted she breathe; babied her with advice.

The breath he ordered arrived: shallow, inadequate.

The passing of cars vibrated her heart.

for Sachiko Murakami

MOVIE OF YOU

In my movie of you, you speak less.
Eye contact is a contract you make good on.
You look at me more, and let me digress.

Edgewise, my words squeeze in,
gather dust and practice poor posture.
In my movie of you, you speak less.

As it's my movie, you obey
the directions I provide;
you look at me more and I can digress.

As you give them importance, my opinions bloat;
you need them for your performance.
In my movie of you, you speak less.

You haunt the props table,
vie for a generous edit.
In my movie of you, you speak less,
you look at me more, and let me digress.

EPITHALAMIUM

The clock in Munich's centre
is adorned with a jester;
knights stab him
in time to bell chimes.

The knights' swords pierce and exit.
Though the jester knows the danger
of close quarters,
his smile does not change.

The building's plaque does not explain the attack.
Every hour invites happy murder.
My husband reddened;
the cross of sweat on his shirt swelled.

The jester readied himself
for another glad assault.
I felt under my blouse
for a ready-made wound receptacle.

ON TRANSLATION

These false legs
whipped around,
de-bone themselves.

Blur. Two eyebrows to one.
An infection entered
invisibly; seeped out like a shadow.

The hole in her nose becomes
the hole in the world.

Pearl necklace received
cedes to music crescendo
piano fingers lose bones.

Press harder
the brush loses paint,
makes a perforated stroke.

Yield to something loungey
at the next landing strip.
Learn German to audit
big boob anal mature dialogue.

Interim translation notes of big boob anal mature:
hear seafood sounds.
heresy wood hounds

hair see lewd mounds
her silly coned rounds

discarded porn names
de-guarded horn games

accustomed to the misheard
a bosomed miss, sheered

chinese crested leg crux
her knees nested in his tux

she wheeze with egg flux
he flees when wig mucks

Page goes blank. Invents a silent moment.

DATE

the scotch's age
ages the relationship
distilled. Sandpaper tongue pursues
a moist spot in her.
What she consumes
makes her consumable.
His palate for the plate
of her belly
potholed at its centre.

envy

DESIGNER

Pay by the fleck, here, on *Champs-Élysées*,
"breathtaking" implies grandiose
 and in his flagship store
 meters are piled
 over a hundred high. The stairs
 are designed
            for ease of climb;
            they induce a deliberate stride.

He smiles when he remembers
people drink from taps.

What was across the street, he purchased,
had demolished,
for a better view of the sky's line.

In such surroundings, liberation
from one's assets is a delight.

for Sarah Steinberg

FRIEDA

Smith College humbly requests access
to what dresses her mother
left. She mustn't impede their plan
to parse material's memory.

Like all royal children, she pretends
to be unwatched. Like all daughters,
she's sick of being compared to her mother.

Fingers poised to respond
pinch a pen, the other hand pins paper to table.
The blackened margin proves
her pen tends to doodle.

It outlines her mother's
profile. What of it? Her grasp of him
irrelevant to academia's
stacked harvest.

Too slim to be called a stack, her output:
each poem wants work, whines
for a title, another title, demands a line
break. Subversive punctuation, something.

MUSE

The silence of her slumber
the inconsequence of her banter
her ponytail a pendulum
the swing swing batter batter.

Corroborator of my personal dictionary.
Transmitter of plotlines,
she flattens her voice to a baritone
when the villain enters.

for Rachelle Hecht

THE FIRST LADY OF COUNTRY MUSIC

Threatened with the Living Legend award
the conscripted tears did not come.
She thanked her mother for her lungs.

She was said to be a stranger to flat notes.
Flattened on the couch, she was her own widow.

Death, no matter the cost, describe it as rest.

13 VARIATIONS ON A THEME
BY ANSELM HÜTTENBRENNER

Schubert wore his wire-rimmed spectacles

to bed. What was he so eager to see?

His invisible handsomeness

Anselm made notorious. So, not his own

face then. Unless he was that eager

to spectate any headway, head wise. Afraid

of the dark, another possible

motive. Or, that efficient,

he wanted to save the gestures

involved in donning and removing

the necessary apparatus.

THE BEAR

Grabbed a tree. Hunched in the river.
Bedded in pine needles. Nosed
a place for himself.

The bear bristled, rigid. Arthritic. Back rubbed
against tree. Processes eliminated. Paws no longer
overhead.

The bear became static. Silent. At risk.
The bear pawed a tree under
a cottage lamp. Weaseled his way onto

a child's bed. Molted and grew a coat of nylon and was tagged
with a warning against excess
heat. The bear was squeezed and did not squeeze.

this page left intentionally blank

wrath

"So what is wrong with one more sin?"
—The Scorpions, "Rock You Like a Hurricane"

SLOW SLICING

Ling Chi (or *Leng T'che*) translated as the *slow process*,
the *lingering death*, or *death by a thousand cuts*

the condemned person is killed using a knife to
    methodically remove
portions of the body over an extended period of time.

Ling Chi translated as *death*.
a knife over time
portions the body.

The term língchí derives from a classical description of
    ascending a mountain, slowly.

                mountain.

      a

                            slowly.

    classically.
The term língchí derives from a description of ascending

describes

a mountain

slowly

                                                  knifed
                                                  by
                                                  time.

descending. Slowly.

Lingchi was reserved for crimes viewed
as especially severe, such as treason or killing one's parents.

especially severe
crimes viewed
on a knife.

Western sensibilities assuaged in 1895 when GE Morrison
    reported, the slicing

is performed after death.

The jury is out   on the mountain
on whether morphine increased or decreased pain. Eyes sliced
first. Psychological agony presumed to be worsened thusly.

Slow slicing was criminalized in 1905. There. There.

PHOTOGRAPH

"…Now we squirm into sarcophagal positions, every
word screaming eat me, bury me, scatter me, and every so often, read my poems.
I'd said I was both hearthfire and holocaust…"
—Rob Allen, *Standing Wave*

His death made footnotes of his friends:
it was Katherine Hepburn
who recalled holocaust's small h meaning to him.
"To burn whole," a rewritten word
towed into *Standing Wave.*

Sunglassed author photo;
a grin glad to be re-read.
I called him the Keith Richards
of Canadian Poetry. He blamed the sun,
diffused my accusation.

He opted for cremation,
could not abide his body grounded,
he welcomed the speed of burning
decomposition even slower than composition—

My photo, a flash of light
and pull of film, arrested
his unglassed eyes,
surfaced by the drawer's tide
arrests me.

THE FEMALE CUCKOLD

after Lucian Freud's *Night Portrait*

Thick round waffles, her husband recalls;
balls and breasts, she hears. Sausages,
more than he could eat, scraped through
egg yolk, that forfeited reproduction,

bulbous toes she sees, brazenly gazing
out the curtain's crack, the cracks that create
the fork's tines. She withholds reaction
when he slips and tells of breakfast

wines, her forehead unlined, her lips passive.
She wonders aloud what secret
ingredient she could try to make her own
waffles so fluffy. He eggs her on with cream

whipped to matchless stiffness.
Her regret at his leaving so much of the menu
unsampled outdoes his own.
He assures her he will go again and sample more.

The right food would've revived his appetite, she counters.
Such feasts are known to be celebrations.
Though he restricts his pleasures to business hours
she remembers sheets cast artificial night
on a mattress.

TO DO

Assume	a standing position
Be	seen
Clean	teeth
Die	
Eat	carbohydrates as available
Forget	someone's name
Go	to work
Help	yourself
Ignore	someone
Judge	
Keep	your hands to yourself.
Locomote	
Manage	expectations
Neglect	your inferiors
Organize	this list
Pretend	you don't see someone
Quiet	your rage
Re-organize	this list
See	
Tamper	with what actually happened
Understand	yourself
Validate	your feelings
Welcome	those that thank you
Xerox	your buttocks
You're	welcome
Zip	up

BODY POLITICIAN

Each body will be represented by one part
penis jumps up to volunteer
dismissed, too obvious, already too persuasive.

Consider the part most often kissed. Or least.
You think you attract attention but it is your jacket.
No matter, it is not eligible.

Your cheek is not such a one the adjective names.
As parts, your ears do not stand out.
Your ass brought you all the love you've ever received,

though it is more cheerleader than spokesperson.
Your nose plays at captain but steers a path only as it must.
Almost forgotten, proves your lips have always been
    unremarkable.

Make a beast of burden your least favourite part
punish the fingerprints for holding you to your crimes.
Remind your heart of its lack of judgment.

A fingernail can be cut and replaced at will.
An eyelash when lost is seldom found.
The gut with its dimple. Impertinent heel.

Not all quarters will hear a nipple
out. Undecided votes will be counted as
the collarbone, or whatever everyone else chooses.

TRIPLETS IN THEIR BEDROOM, N.J., 1963

after Diane Arbus

I

Made of shadow
Her shadow is a second attempt

One works in a grenade factory. The others
in the toy grenade factory.

Repetitive motion syndrome:
repeating their own motions, and each others.

Filed under iconic photograph.

2

Some think they
favour one another
over other siblings.

3

Yes, the triplets have
dreamed in triplicate.

One wonders what it would be like if there were two.
Four. If only one, would it be her?
If it wasn't, she would know.

She can tell the girls who wish they had copies.

[HIS SUBJECT NEEDED AN UMBRELLA]

"Painting," 1946 Francis Bacon

His subject needed an umbrella
more than a head

(rain?)

some works withheld from the public
Every painting slashed was—

a fine grade of canvas
no primer

The paints glide
decline the illusion of depth

A sound does not admit its origin
Smear suggests movement

withheld from the public
every painting was slashed

AFTERWORD

"THIS LAND DOES GO ON FOREVER"

—Kathleen Olmstead

Slumming at sea level, the highway
kept mum the mystery
of those who had built it.

Fewer radio stations than towns.
From the shoulder sheet aluminum shouts
their names; a stranger born in each of them.

The pictogram fork-and-knife framed teacup
reminds you all you ever needed to know
about disappointment is only ever an exit away.

The highway is too straight, then not straight enough.
I dip onto the shoulder; it dips into me.
The weather keeps me company.

Thank you Mom. Thank you Eva Moran, Angela
Szczepaniak, David McGimpsey, Rachelle Hecht, Sachiko
Murakami, Angela Rawlings, Paul Vermeersch, Jake
Mooney, Spencer Gordon, J Lemieux, Kathleen Olmstead,
and Margaret Geri Kingston.

Thanks are due to Palimpsest Press and Insomniac Press
through the Ontario Council for the Arts, Writer's Reserve.
Thank you to Canada Council for the Arts Mid Career
Writers Grant and the Joseph S. Stauffer prize.

Thank you to the editors of the following journals:

"Law Of Similarity" appeared in *Event* (Vol. 41, Issue 1
    Summer 2012)

"Photograph" and "Sorrow Machine" appeared in *Descant*
    (Vol. 43, Issue 157, Summer 2012)

"Formula (for Everything)" appeared in *Toronto Poetry
    Vendors* (Issue 2, 2012)

"Reality Checklist" appeared in *ditch*

"Bones" and "Movie of You" appeared in puritan-magazine.com
    (Issue 8, Fall 2009)

"On Translation" appeared in *Matrix* (Issue #85, Spring 2010)

"13 Variations on a theme by Anselm Hüttenbrenner" and
    "Milk" appeared in *Contemporary Verse 2* (Spring 2013)

"Triplets in their bedroom, NJ, 1963" appeared in the
    puritan-magazine.com (Issue XXII, Summer 2013)

"Poem in place of a trip to Niagara Falls" appeared in
    decompmagazine.com (July 2013)

"Epithalamium" appeared in smokinggluegun.com
    (Volume 7, September 2013)

"Bariatric Surgery," "Slow Slicing," and "The Fitzgeralds
    on Leave" appeared in PANKmagazine.com
    (December 2013)

"Light Detection" and "Francis Bacon's Studio" appeared in thewritingdisorder.com (2013)

"CHOOSE YOUR FAVOURITE SHAPE and "Body Politician" appeared in rustytoque.com (Issue 7, Winter 2014)

Bibliography

Dyson, Michael Eric. *Pride* (Oxford University Press, 2005).

Espaillat, Rhina P. "Find Work" in *Poetry Magazine* (Chicago, February 1999).

Olmstead, Kathleen. "Seasonal wishes from Northern Quebec" in *Taddle Creek* (Vitalis Publishing, 1999).

Thurman, Robert, A.F. *Anger* (Oxford University Press, 2006).

Tickle, Phyllis, A. *Greed* (Oxford University Press, 2004).

Wasserstein, Wendy. *Sloth* (Oxford University Press, 2005).

Zapruder, Matthew. *Come On All You Ghosts* (Copper Canyon Press, c2010).

Angela Hibbs is the author of two previous collections of poetry, *Passport* (DC Books, 2006) and *Wanton* (Insomniac Press, 2009). She holds a MA creative writing from Concordia University. Her work appeared in the Poetry Is Public Is Poetry installation at the Toronto Reference Library. She was awarded the 2010 Joseph S. Stauffer Prize.